1 MONTH OF FREE READING

at

www.ForgottenBooks.com

By purchasing this book you are eligible for one month membership to ForgottenBooks.com, giving you unlimited access to our entire collection of over 1,000,000 titles via our web site and mobile apps.

To claim your free month visit:

www.forgottenbooks.com/free903886

* Offer is valid for 45 days from date of purchase. Terms and conditions apply.

ISBN 978-0-266-88144-5
PIBN 10903886

This book is a reproduction of an important historical work. Forgotten Books uses state-of-the-art technology to digitally reconstruct the work, preserving the original format whilst repairing imperfections present in the aged copy. In rare cases, an imperfection in the original, such as a blemish or missing page, may be replicated in our edition. We do, however, repair the vast majority of imperfections successfully; any imperfections that remain are intentionally left to preserve the state of such historical works.

Forgotten Books is a registered trademark of FB &c Ltd.
Copyright © 2018 FB &c Ltd.
FB &c Ltd, Dalton House, 60 Windsor Avenue, London, SW19 2RR.
Company number 08720141. Registered in England and Wales.

For support please visit www.forgottenbooks.com

ANNUAL CATALOGUE OF
GOOD FIELD SEEDS
FROM

SPRING 1901

J.C. SUFFERN
SPECIALTY SEED GROWER

CHAMPION YELLOW DENT

EXACT SIZE OF SEEDS

WHITE BEAUTY SUNFLOWER.

ORIGINATED BY J. C. SUFFERN

CHANGE YOUR SEED

Some farmers keep sowing old run-out varieties, because they have the seed handy. They do not figure up their loss by so doing.

WHEN LETTERS are mailed in Ohio, Indiana, Missouri, and Kansas, to-day, fast mail generally delivers them to me on to-morrow.

HON. ISAAC MORTON said "That the product of one quart of a variety of wheat brought from North Carolina in 1845, had in nine years benefitted the farmers of Preble county, O., alone, more than $100,000.00 by the gain over what they would have had, if they had continued raising the old varieties."
Address

J. C. Suffern
SEED GROWER
VOORHIES   ILLINOIS.

DROUTH BEATING CORN—SEE PAGE 7.

MY RESPONSIBILITY.

Confidence is the foundation of all business transactions. That is just what I want,—*your* confidence. My previous record entitles me to it. I ask your fullest investigation of my reputation in the past, my financial standing at the present time, and my ability to perform what I promise in the future. If you have never yet ordered seeds from me, then you naturally desire to know whether it is safe to send me money. And you have a right to know. I refer you for information to (in making inquiries, always enclose stamped envelope addressed to yourself, for their reply to your inquiry): First National Bank, Bement, Illinois. Postmaster, Voorhies, Ill. Pacific Express Agent, Voorhies, Ill.

DIRECTIONS FOR ORDERING.

ORDER EARLY. And then you will be sure to have the seed just when you want it. Send your order to-day. Before you lose my address. Unless my trade is very much larger than I expect, I will have plenty of seed of the varieties herein advertised until June 15th.

MY TERMS are **strictly cash with the Order.** Send money by registered letter, money order, or by Chicago or New York draft. At my risk. Money order office, Voorhies, Illinois. No seed sent C. O. D. Personal checks on country banks not wanted, as it costs me 20 cents each to collect them. Express money orders for sale at all express offices, are cheap, and very safe.

SHIPPING. I am located on the Wabash and I. D. & W. R'ys. Midway between Chicago and St. Louis. The Wabash R'y reaches Toledo, Detroit, Indianapolis, Chicago, St. Louis, Kansas City, and Omaha. Be sure and state what route you wish seeds sent by. When no instructions are given, I shall use my best judgment in the matter.

THIS PRICE LIST. Do you wish to receive it regularly, from time to time, as it comes forth? If so, you must write me to that effect. As I am continually revising my list of addresses. And do not wish to mail it to any one to whom it is of no use. Please show it to your neighbors, and then put it away with your valuable papers. So you can get it quickly, when you wish to order. Tell all your friends about my seeds. And get them to order with you. If this price list should become misplaced, or lost, write at once, for another copy, which will be sent in haste. If you do not receive my 1899 Catalogue, you can order from this one, as prices will be about the same.

WARRANTING. While I exercise the greatest care to have all my seeds pure and reliable, it is hereby mutually agreed between myself and the purchaser, that I do not warrant any of my seeds. And am not in any respect, liable or responsible for the seeds sold by me. Or for any failure thereof in any respect. Of course I sell seeds of good vitality. And as pure as the greatest care can keep them. See page 7.

SEAMLESS BAGS. Send 15c (worth 20c.) extra for a new extra heavy seamless bag, in which to ship each 2 bushels or less, of seed that you order.

Express or Freight Charges always to be paid by purchaser.

For Large Quantities, or price on an assortment, write for special prices.

I Guarantee Safe arrival of the seed at your station. Do not forget to remit for sacks.

REDUCED FREIGHT CHARGES. In the past it has been the general practice of railroad companies, to charge about twice as much for hauling seed grain as for market grain. At a recent meeting of the General Official Classification Committee, in New York City, of all railroads, the charges on seed grain were lowered all over the country, to that of ordinary market grain. So now it will cost about one half as much as heretofore to ship seed corn, wheat, oats, etc.

I advise my customers to have their seeds sent by freight. As it is much cheaper than by express. I can generally reach most points in Ohio, Tennessee and Kansas, in three to eight days, and in Indiana, Missouri and Kentucky, in three to six days. By freight from here. I cannot send to a station which has no freight agent, as the freight charges must be prepaid to such stations. In such cases I advise you to order me to send it to nearest station to you which has an agent. Please give me the name of your nearest Railroad. Also how far, and what direction you are from the nearest of the cities named in the "freight rates." I guarantee safe arrival of the seeds at your station.

MY SELECTION. Many of my customers send me $5, $10, $20, up to $50, and request me to send them the worth of their money in corn, oats, or wheat, best suited to their soils, or to their localities. My knowledge of what varieties do best on particular soils or in particular localities, has been obtained by my personal visits to many localities, and by the report of my customers in all parts of the country. If you desire that I make selections for you, then please state in your order the character of your soil. Whether it is hard pan, sandy, red clay, brown, black, limestone, alkali, red shale, post oak, upland or lowland. And I will give you the most that I can for the cash you send, of the best varieties for your soil.

In filling orders we carefully label each kind, inside of the bags, so you will know them when you get them.

RAPID TRANSIT. I have rapid transit arrangements to many points. And with my system of tracing, I have greatly lessened delays in the transit of my shipments.

The past spring I succeeded in reaching most Texas points in seven to twelve days. Most Louisiana points in six to ten days, and most Georgia points in seven to twelve days. It is always important to you to get your seed through quickly. You may rest assured that I will always use every means in my power to hurry your seeds through with the least possible delay in transit. I now put 2 or 3 Foster's Commercial tracers after each shipment. Delays are thereby quickly discovered, and the seeds pushed through with the least possible delay in transit. A well-known Georgia Seed Co., recently wrote me thus: "Please ship us the following additional order. Tracing in your usual energetic and effective manner."

BUY YOUR SEEDS OF THE GROWER.

I acknowledge all orders, as soon as received. And notify my customers when I ship their seeds.

P 3

SUFFERNS' SEED ORDER SHEET

Name	Amount Enclosed
P. O.	$ ....
Co. .... State	Please state whether in Cash, Stamps, Money Order or Draft.
Freight Station	
Railroad	....
Send Seeds by	Date .... 189..

Plain letter paper can be used for larger orders.

If we are sold out of any of the articles which your order on this sheet, are you willing for us to substitute anything of equal value and habit? Yes, or No ....
See bottom of page 2, and center of page 5.

IN MAKING YOUR ORDERS, PLEASE STATE THE PRICE

BUS.	NAMES OF SEEDS WANTED	PRICE TOTALS.
		DOLLARS. | CENTS.
......	CHAMPION YELLOW DENT CORN	|
......	CHAMPION WHITE PEARL CORN	|
......	IMPROVED LEAMING CORN	|
......	RED BEAUTY POP CORN	|
......	MONARCH WHITE RICE POP CORN	|

CARRIED FORWARD.
OVER.

BUS.	NAMES OF SEEDS WANTED	CARRIED FORWARD	PRICE TOTALS.	
			DOLLS	CENTS.
	New Seamless Bags	at 15 cents each		

TERMS STRICTLY CASH   GRAND TOTAL

NO GOODS SENT C. O. D. Under any circumstances. Please don't ask it; extra work for us and needless expense to our patrons.

PLEASE WRITE BELOW, THE NAMES AND POST OFFICE OF YOUR FRIENDS WHOM YOU HAVE KNOWN TO SEND OFF FOR FIELD SEEDS

NAME	POST OFFICE	STATE

Extra Order Sheets will be mailed upon application. Buy your seeds of the grower.

I Guarantee Safe arrival of the seed at your station. Do not forget to remit for sacks, 15c each.

In Your Orders, please state second choice, in case I am out of your first choice.

A YOUNG MAN is full of life and vigor, when an old man is about ready to go to that bourne from which no traveler ever returns. So also of old and new varieties of wheat, oats, corn, etc.

Don't forget to ask your neighbor to join you in sending for some of our good varieties of seeds.

MY INCREASED TRADE

During the past six years, my trade has more than quadrupled over the six preceding years.
My largest order came from a club of farmers in Adams County, Ills., for $276.30. Next largest from Neosho Co., Kansas, $117.50. Next largest from Smith Co., Tenn., for $105.45. Next largest from Posey Co., Ind., for $78.47. Next largest from Hickory County Mo., for $74.35. Next largest from Tippecanoe Co., for $65.88. Next largest from Brown Co., Ills., for $64.61. Next largest from Adams Co., Ill., for $62.00. Next largest from Bedford Co., Tenn., for $56.00. Next largest from St. Charles Co., Mo., for $55.00. Next largest from Grant Co., Ky., for $54.00. Next largest from Hancock Co., Ills., for $53.75, and so on. I am fully prepared this spring, for a much larger trade than I expect. Help form a club in your locality, and send me a large order, and make the price of seed 10 times over, in your largely increased yield. Don't put it off until next spring, order now.

TWENTIETH CENTURY INTRODUCTION.

At the dawn of the new century, a bright new era in cereal breeding is being ushered in. Taking a retrospective view of human achievements during the century just closed, wonderful, awe-inspiring, indeed, they have been, in almost every department of human endeavor.

Progress in bending material things to man's needs and fancies, especially in the mechanical and live stock pursuits, has simply eclipsed individual vision. In view of the rapid advancement that has been made during the past 50 years, in the improvement of our domesticated animals, through the efforts of skilful breeders, regretful in the extreme it must be, that there has been such little progress in breeding our grain-bearing plants with a view to steadily increasing yield.

In view of the disgracefully low average yields of all of our grain-bearing plants, it is a fact beyond dispute, that until very recent years, the efforts of cereal breeders (if they could be termed such) have been for the most part unsystematic and intermittent. Little wonder that as farmers have been fast depleting our virgin soil, that the average yields of our important cereal crops should steadily decline. But, happily, as the wheels of progress are now being oiled by a generation of born cereal breeders, they have begun to rapidly revolve in the direction of steady and surprising increases in the average yields of our cereal plants.

The writer (and other young cereal breeders) is devoting life to cereal breeding in all of its numerous phases; and after 28 years' practical field experience as a seed grower, I firmly believe that prior to the year 1925, as the science of cereal breeding becomes more thoroughly understood, and much more intensely practiced, that the increase in our average yields of the grain-bearing plants will be almost beyond human computation. And that the degree of perfection that will be attained in the not far distant future by ingenious seed and plant breeders, in the continued improvement of our cereals, vegetables, and flowers, will cause the glad earth to pour out her blessings to the husbandman in far greater abundance in the way of maximum yields than has ever yet been dreamed of by our most progressive men. The writer firmly believes that our low average yields of important cereal crops is due in a far greater degree than most farmers imagine to the habit of barrenness and its attendant degeneracy—dry rot, smut, low germinating power, and general organic weakness; and that skillful plant breeders will so decrease the habit of barrenness, by well-balanced breeding pressure, during the next few years, that our average yields will be much more than doubled. Blowhard, Fast & Co. are one of a certain class of seed firms who annually prey upon the credulity of the average farmer by the introduction of a host of so-called wonderful novelties, claimed to have been discovered by chance on board of an abandoned ship in the Indian Ocean, or in a bag of coffee in South America, or in some antiquated Indian mound, or in some other mysterious manner, and which is invariably offered under high-sounding names, and sold under inflated, extravagant claims. Such dealers are little better than highway robbers.

Ingenious man can never hope to successfully make silk purses from sows' ears. Neither can he expect financial gain from patronizing such firms as Blowhard, Fast & Co.

God forbid that the writer should ever stoop to such underhand methods of securing trade. It is my constant aim to only breed, grow, and offer varieties of cereals which have a freedom from barrenness and a buoyantly adaptive constitution, and which will be an actual financial gain to my customers.

And many thousand customers throughout the land who like price and quality well balanced show their faith in my seeds, by continued and increasing patronage. Trusting to be favored with your correspondence and early orders, and wishing one and all a prosperous year, meantime,
Yours anxious to please,

Telegraph address, Bement, Ill.
January 1, 1901.
Established 1882.

J. C. SUFFERN,
VOORHIES, ILLINOIS.

YOUR SECOND AND THIRD CHOICE | Buy your seeds of the grower.

During the course of a large trade, it sometimes happens that the demand for some particular variety, or varieties, is unexpectedly large, and soon exhausts my stock of it. While I will continue to have a good supply of other varieties until close of season. If it happens that I am sold out of part or all of what you order, it will be a great time saver to us both, and will prevent delay and disappointment if you will state in your order, (or make your next choice.) If I may send a variety which I may consider **as good, or about as good, or better**, for your soil, (state what kind of soil you have), than what you order. And if the variety which I may send you, is lower priced than what you order, I will refund difference. If it is higher priced, will put it to you at the same price per bu. as the one you ordered. Or if you do not wish any but the kind you order, please state if I may order some good reliable Seed Co., to fill your order, with the same variety, at no extra cost to you. Or if you wish your money returned, I will do so. **Be sure to instruct me in regard to the above.**

SUFFERN'S SEEDS ARE GROWN BY SUFFERN.

FREIGHT RATES.—For the benefit of my customers, to save them time in writing about how much freight charges will be on a certain quantity of seed, I here quote you rates to 28 large cities. From the rate named to the city nearest you, you can draw an idea of about what the charges will be before you order. At distant points—500 to 800 miles, the charges will be at least 50c on quantities of seed grain to amount of 100 lbs. or less. See bottom of page 2.

Rates on seed grain in bags, per 100 lbs., at this date, from Voorhies, Ills., to—

Atchison, Kan........32c	Cedar Rapids, Ia.....24c	Louisville, Ky........19c	Richmond, Va........33c
Atlanta, Ga..........42c	Detroit, Mich.........12c	Milwaukee, Wis......26c	Rockford, Ills........17c
Bowling Green, Ky...32c	East St. Louis, Ills...17c	Memphis, Tenn......31c	St. Paul, Minn.......28c
Buffalo, N. Y........20c	Evansville, Ind.......15c	Mobile, Ala...........37c	Sioux City, Ia........28c
Chicago, Ill..........17c	Indianapolis, Ind.....11c	Macon, Ga............44c	Terre Haute, Ind.....10c
Cincinnati, Ohio.....15c	Kansas City, Mo......32c	Nashville, Tenn......37c	Toronto, Canada.....20c
Council Bluffs, Ia....32c	Lincoln, Neb..........36c	New Orleans, La.....22c	Vicksburg, Miss......23c

BIG CROPS, AND HOW TO PRODUCE THEM.

In the European countries, intensive cultivation is pursued far more intensely than in America. Here the system of farming (if system it can be called,) is often conducted on happy-go-lucky methods. Consequently our cultivated lands as a whole, rarely produce scarcely half as much as they might. In the grain producing industry of this great country, the question constantly crowding upon the attention of all enterprising up to date farmers and land owners is: "How can I secure the largest yield." Every farmer quickly admits that a big yield on a small acreage, is always more profitable, than a large acreage with only a moderate yield. It stands to reason that he is most prosperous who gets most from a given area. Then expenses do not increase in proportion to the yield. The added outlay comes when we go to increasing the area to get the increased yield desired. The bottom's out of farming in the old ways. Low prices can't be met by harder work,—you've got to change your methods. Raise double the crops on the same land, with less work. Can't be done? it *is* done!

The low prices warn us that we must raise larger crops on the same ground and with the same labor or our farming will not Pay. Nothing assists so much in growing the largest crops as to sow or plant the best seed. If 35 bushels of corn per acre will pay expenses of growing; if you can get 50 bushels per acre you will have 15 bushels per acre for profit, while if you only get 35 bushels you have no profit.

Progress is the leading characteristic of this age. The old is rapidly being replaced by the new and improved. It is truly wonderful to witness the progress that has been made in the way of increased yields in cereals, corn, and potatoes the past twenty years. It has become a well known fact to all good farmers, that our older varieties of cereals are continually running out. And that a change of seed is very important, in order to secure good crops. Those varieties known 100 years ago are forgotten. And those grown 25 years ago, are now nearly entirely out of cultivation. Whoever may have noticed, when the Fultz, Lancaster, Red Mediterranean, and Clauson Wheats were first introduced in the West, from the Eastern States, have seen, that in many instances their yields were almost double those of the older varieties then grown. After having produced several good crops, they too, have almost run out. And are fast going the same road that al the old varieties go, so it is with other grain.

In this age of new inventions, old machines, cereals, etc., are continually giving way to new and improved ones. In one short life, we can see the practical developments of human ingenuity. And become convinced, that we are not only subject to laws of gradual advancement, but that our forward strides in the Sciences, Agriculture, and Mechanics, have been great indeed. In this age of keen competition, the farmer who wishes to prosper, needs and gets the most improved farming implements; and by reading the best agricultural literature, he keeps in touch with the spirit of progress that pervades our farming communities. He is particular, also, in regard to the kind of seed he plants and the manner of planting it.

Indeed, the profit of grain production depends, to a great extent, on growing the right varieties. there being thousands of instances where eighty to one hundred bushels of the best quality of corn per acre might just as well be grown as thirty to forty bushels of a poorer quality if only the right varieties were grown. The old, run-out sorts which you have been growing, perhaps, for many years, should be dropped, and a stock of vigorous, new, thoroughbred varieties obtained. After you have tried them, you will see plainly that they are as much superior in every way to the old run out sorts as are thoroughbred cattle to scrubs.

Thoroughbred cereals, especially the most highly bred of these, whose organic relations are so harmonious and plastic, and whose flexibility of organization has been so highly developed through the intervention of skillful breeders, are being continually transported from one part of the world to another, with the greatest success. Breeders have "moulded," by systematic mating and selection, an extraordinary inherent flexible and prepotent constitution which yields gracefully to changed conditions of life-soil, climate, altitude, etc. And changed conditions of life seem to be of the highest importance in favorably affecting the productive powers, by directly acting on this flexible organization. The greater or less force of organic flexibility determines how productive or profitable a plant will be under changed conditions of soil and climate. If it is the possessor of a low organization, in which atavism or reversion is annually out-cropping, it will more or less suffer under changed conditions, as regards its productive capacity, owing to action of new chemical soil properties, proximity to bodies of water, mountain ranges, new insect depredators, etc.

Farmers desirous of changing their seed should exercise the utmost care to procure only thoroughbred seed, to insure safe and sure increases in yields. The seed is parent of the plant, and bounds its possibilities. So critical an observer as the noted Dr. E. Lewis Sturtevent has given facts on which he rests a belief that the kind of used is capable of making as wide a difference in the crop as manured against unmanured land. And experienced farmers, who judiciously change their seed, have often noticed the same fact. To secure the best seed is of more importance to the farmer, and to the country generally, than it is to secure the best live stock. The plant precedes the animal, and its cost modifies the cost of animal products. It is an undisputed fact that the laws governing breeding are as potent in plant as in animal life, and respond as fully to the breeder's art. The successful plant breeder is never satisfied with what he has already attained. But, like the expert inventor of mechanical devices, he is continually striving for something better.

Hon. Isaac Morton said that "the product of one quart of a variety of wheat brought from North Carolina, in 1845, has benefitted the farmers of Preble county, Ohio, alone, more than $1000,000 by the gain over what they would have had if they had continued to raise the old, run-out varieties."

A young man is full of life and vigor when an old man is about ready to go to that bourne from which no traveller ever returns. So also of old and new varieties of wheat, oats, corn, etc. Every old farmer can recall varieties that yielded abundantly in his younger days, but are out of cultivation now and their names almost forgotten. Of several varieties of corn that may be tried on any particular soil, one will yield almost double what some other will. The same is true of hardiness and other qualities. It pays big to get fresh seed from a different locality and soil (it seems almost a new being coming forth from the corpse of an old one), even if it be only the same old variety which you have been growing. A vigorous, hardy new variety will produce a good crop, in an unfavorable year, while a run-out tender variety seldom produces a satisfactory crop under most favorable conditions.

It will cost you only about twenty-five cents per acre to plant your whole crop with the vigorous, large-yielding new sorts of corn. And I can safely say that if you get the right sorts, your yield will be greatly increased and in many instances doubled. This has been the experience of the writer during many years of active farming. Let each farmer consider what an increased yield of one, two, five or ten bushels per acre on each acre of corn, wheat or oats he grows, will amount to and then *how much money and time he can afford to spend to obtain these results.* Owing to the superior yield that will be realized with my varieties of wheat, corn, oats, etc., it will pay to plant largely of them, to raise for the general market even at the price given.

In a letter just received from a gentleman in Central Missouri, he says: "I am satisfied that my yield has been increased at least one-third by changing my seed corn." Ask a German farmer what he thinks about changing seed, and he will almost invariably tell you that he believes in it, and believes in it strongly. At least, he was so brought up in Germany, in which country it is practised to a greater extent than any other country in the world.

J. C. SUFFERN.

Voorhies, Illinois.

DROUTH BEATING CORN.

According to the most reliable southern authority, the largest corn that can be well matured in the heart of the great Illinois corn belt, if well-bred, and grown not less than three stalks per hill, matures a good yield of corn in the south twenty to thirty days before the horrid, death-dealing hot winds or early drouth catches and ruins the native corn, this also applies to Kansas. See proof below.

"Man was made for dominion over all the earth," says the good book. And he is improving his opportunities these latter days by placing all known forces of nature under contribution for his benefit. Civilized and enlightened man is continually inventing and unfolding new methods for shortening labor, saving time, enhancing the value of and cheapening the cost of his productions. By his ingenuity he out-generals the otherwise disastrous effects of adverse seasons, circumvents the attacks of injurious insects, and supplies the defects of natural production by artificial production. In the carrying out of his various enterprises he draws upon all parts of the earth for assistance.

At the present day we see that European and North American varieties of grain have been introduced into, and almost entirely occupy the grain growing lands of Argentina, New Zealand, Chili, and many oceanica countries. In some cases an imported variety of grain is at its best only after it has become acclimated. While other varieties, or other species best fulfill the purpose intended, as regards yield texture, flavor, etc, during their first year's growth in their new home. Thereafter annually decreasing in yield, flavor, or texture as they become gradually acclimated. In order for Kansas farmers to most successfully produce the noted "Kansas Hard Milling Wheat," which is becoming so popular in the world's great markets, fresh importations of unacclimated seed must frequently be made from the Crimean country, near the eastern end of the Mediterranean Sea. For as the very hard Crimean wheat becomes acclimated in Kansas, it has during the process of acclimation, gradually degenerated into a soft wheat.

The market gardeners of New England in order to produce their profitable Cauliflower crops must import their seed from far off Holland. The truck farmer of the cotton states in order to produce his very profitable cabbage crops, is compelled to often renew his seed stock from the cold north, for when cabbage becomes thoroughly acclimated in the south, it has then degenerated into the sprangly, loose-headed collard. The largest growing latest maturing varieties of northern corn yield much the best in the cotton states during drouthy seasons. On the other hand, varieties of wheat and oats from states further south, yield best in Illinois, and other northern states. The much larger yield obtained from Texas Red Rustproof Oats, in a comparative test of many northern and southern varieties of oats, at the Illinois Experiment Station, Urbana, Illinois, helps bear me out in this assertion.

There are many southern farmers who harbor the idea that northern grown corn must be acclimatized in the south before the best yields can be secured from it. But the writer's experience (supported by many southern experimenters') is directly the reverse. The right kind (thoroughbred) of northern corn produces its best yield in the south during the first year of its growth there. Thereafter annually decreasing in yield as it becomes acclimatized. For while it is becoming acclimatized, it gradually acquires the large stalk and late maturity of the southern native corn, until it loses its great value as a drouth beater. The southern native corn also gradually loses its great value as a fodder producer in the far north, during the process of its acclimatization to the cold northern climate.

I could give many more such instances along this line, but suffice it to say that every country under the sun is deficient in some manner, and in certain years, as regards crop production, and man is to a great extent meeting and supplying these deficiencies by his ingenious experiments. In this connection, I will here mention what a great boon it is to the farmers of the northern states and Canada, that the large-growing, succulent and abundant fodder-producing dent corns from the cotton states have been so generally adopted there to fill the gap of their naturally deficient forage production. It is a boon that is annually worth many millions of dollars to the cold northern country, with its short growing seasons.

An otherwise great west and south agriculturally, is in very many years greatly hampered in the matter of corn production by the oft-recurring hot winds and early drouths. What an equally great boon it is to the corn growers of the cotton states, also including Kansas, that early maturing varieties of corn from Illinois are to a large extent displacing the cultivation of the large native southern corn. It is boon indeed. A no less valuable one financially than is the importation of southern corn and southern-grown millet seed for northern forage production.

The writer having noticed that there has been a lively discussion in several southern agricultural journals during the past year, regarding the relative value of northern corn and southern native corn, for beating hot winds and early drouths with, and that some experimenters had not met with the fullest measure of success in growing northern corn, I will here state that "there is a right way, and a wrong way of doing everything." The farmers who have met with poor success have taken the wrong way. They have planted "run out" extra early northern corn. If the same farmers hitch to the wrong end of their reaper it will not cut their wheat. If you practice the right way success is yours, but if you practice the wrong way, failure is surely yours. Having a largely increased southern trade for Illinois grown corn, I therefore am in a position to condense in this catalogue some facts bearing on the subject, and gathered from reliable southern sources during the past few years. Since it was discovered by enterprising southern experimenters that northern corn transported to the south would work wonders, many grain dealers, as well as uninformed northern seed dealers, have taken advantage of the situation in recommending and supplying the very earliest eight-rowed flint corns, and extra early dent corns from the far north, and poorly bred "run out" dent corns from the middle north, as the best sorts to beat the hot winds and early drouths with. **Early Corn** is what you want. But it must not be **too early.** As "too much of anything is often good for nothing." If the northern corn is too early, then too much of your growing season is wasted between the time of its maturity and the beginning of the hot winds and drouth. According to reliable authority in the south the latest varieties of thoroughbred corn that can be matured in the middle north are the best yielding varieties for all localities in the southern states subject to hot winds and drouth. Our late corn here, is not small. It has large ears often fifteen inches long and weighing one and one-half to two pounds.

These are facts in the truest sense of the word, and are substantiated by reports of comparative tests of large numbers of northern and southern varieties of corn at several southern experiment stations and large numbers of intelligent farmers throughout the cotton states and in Kansas. Facts gathered from indisputable sources assure me that northern corn to best succeed in the south must not be **too early,** and it must by all means be well bred – not "run out." The result of a comparative test of sixty-two varieties of northern and southern corn at the Texas Experiment Station, College Station, Texas, in 1896, helps bear me out in this statement. The early maturing corn from the northern states has enabled the farmers of the cotton states to out-general the oft recurring horrid hot winds and death dealing droughts. By their cultivation he now secures fair to good yields grown alongside of the southern native corn that often makes little or nothing. In many localities in the southern states, and in Kansas, the growth of the large growng, late maturing native corn is very often cut short while it is forming its pollen and silk, its pollen often being prematurely dried up during the process of its formation by hot winds or extremely hot atmosphere, and as there naturally can be little grain formation unless preceeded by abundant and mature pollen in the tassel of the corn plant, the product of the southern native corn is often sadly deficient. Thoroughbred, early northern corn, with its inherent flexible and plastic organization, and which often yields (at least in the vicinity of the home of the writer, which is a locality of almost exclusive corn production) 80 to 100 bushels per acre over large fields with ordinary good cultivation, when transported to Texas, Georgia, Louisiana, and other southern states and Kansas, carries its prolificacy and early maturity with it. It has the great advantage of maturing its pollen and ripening its ears twenty to thirty days sooner than the large growing, late maturing native corn planted on the same day, Thus it, to a great extent, escapes the withering rays of "Old Sol" during the most critical period in corn production, thereby producing a fair to good yield of corn of a good quality per acre, while the native corn begins to form its pollen and silk so much later that it is caught by the hot winds and drouth, and in consequence yields little or nothing.

Even within fourteen days often proves to be the critical period of ear formation and maturity, and the whole crop is either ruined or made, just as you plant, native or northern corn. Northern corn to succeed best in the cotton states and Kansas, must also be thoroughbred. Highly bred varieties of cereals, especially the most **thoroughbred** of these whose organic relations are so harmonious and plastic, and whose flexibility, prepotency and vigor of organization have been so highly developed by ingenious breeders, are being continually transported from one part of the world to another, with the most gratifying results. Plant breeders have moulded, by systematic mating and selection, an extraordinary inherent flexible constitution, which yields graceful y and prepotently to changed conditions of soil and climate. The greater or less force of organic flexibility and vigor determining how productive or profitable an animal or plant will be when transported to a different soil or climate. If the seed or plant be a common "run out" cheaply grown sort, the possessor of a weak impotent organization, in which atavism or reversion is continually cut cropping, it will more or less suffer under changed conditions of soil and climate. Its organization being too weak to withstand the shock of so great a change in conditions of soil and climate.

Short corn crops resulting from severe drought, occur in the south about every other year, as a rule. With thoroughbred northern corn you are assured of a fair to good yield, when the large stalk, late maturing southern native corn makes little or nothing. Even during the most favorable years for the southern native corn, just as good yields can be secured from the northern corn grown alongside, from the fact that corn which yields from 80 to 100 bushels per acre over large fields here in Illinois, can, and should be grown just as thickly in the cotton states as it is grown in Illinois (three stalks per hill). The soil of the cotton states maturing three stalks and three good ears of corn grown from Illinois short stalk seed, just as easily as the usual one large stalk and one ear of the southern native corn per hill. Furthermore if still earlier varieties (say ninety day corn) of northern seed corn be planted in the south as early as March 1, they will mature by June 1. Then if the same corn be planted about Aug. 1. of the same year, another crop of it can be matured with the usual fall rains. I have many southern customers to whom I ship corn every summer for planting on wheat and oat stubble.

PRESS COMMENTS.

"As such large sections of this state suffered by severe drouth last season, the early northern seed corn is in great request here this year. Every farmer that is trying to make both ends meet should plant northern corn this spring."—Southern Farmer, New Orleans, La., spring, 1896.

"All our farmers here agree that northern corn beats our native corn. Even last year (1895) it did best. It is a generally admitted fact that northern corn matures much quicker than our native corn. We also get a sounder, healthier grain from the northern corn. Here in the south we should import northern corn every spring. We hope that our drouth sufferers will plant plenty of northern corn this spring."—Monroe Bulletin, Monroe, La., spring. 1896.

"It is much to be regretted, that the corn crop which about the first of June, promised so well, throughout Texas, has been cut short in many sections in the state. Hot winds followed by drouth, did the mischief. We learn from many sources that where northern seed corn was planted in good time, its crop was safe from harm before the drouth reached us. By all means, a portion at least of every farmer's crop should be planted with northern seed corn every spring "—Live Stock and Farm Journal, Ft. Worth, Texas, Aug. 18. 1897.

An editorial in Texas Farm and Ranch, the past summer, says: "Because Texas has been blessed with abundant rains this year, there is no reason to believe that she will be so blessed next year, or year after. We have good crops this year. But how about next year? That we do not have the same abundant rain fall one year with another, should warn the prudent man to look out for dry weather next year."

A clipping from a Southern Agricultural Journal in 1897, says: "The generally poor corn crop in the south this year (1897) should cause planters to study up means to avoid this in the future. The causes of the short corn crops, which, come about every other year here, as a rule, is the careless planting of mixed late native sorts of corn. Only choice selected early varieties whose seed has been grown in the north should be planted here. For the reason that they mature their ears before hot winds or drouth kill southern native corn."

An article in the Kansas Farmer the past summer, written by Geo. L. Clothier, ass't botanist of the Kansas Experiment Station, says:—"I believe a majority of Kansas corn growers are well enough acquainted with Kansas climate to expect a drouth sometime in July or August. While our large growing native varieties of corn will outyield imported early varieties during a wet summer, yet a wet July and August comes so seldom that we can afford to accept the somewhat smaller yield of the early corn in such a year, that we may be assured much higher yields from it in our much more frequent dry summers."

A writer in Kansas Farmer under date of Sept. 6, 1898, asks:—' Why do not Kansas farmers grow more early varieties of corn? Our late native varieties are obliged to run the guantlet of July and August drouth, or hot winds. While early varieties of corn are matured ahead of the drouth and hot winds. At least they are so far advanced toward maturity before July 1, that even with severe drouth thenceforward, a fair to good crop is generally secured from them. This year early varieties of corn are yielding twenty to thirty bushels per acre in Kansas, while the late maturing native varieties growing alongside are yielding less than five bushels per acre. It was just so last year, and it is so as a rule. In a really good corn ye r, which comes in Kansas as often as once in ten years, our large native varieties will yield more corn to the acre. And many farmers gamble on this chance."

♦ In Bulletin No. 75 (page 368) for 1896, published by the Alabama Agricultural Experiment Station, Auburn, Ala., (and which will be sent free to all farmers in Alabama, who will write for it) may be seen the following:—"But it is an interesting fact that in the abnormally dry season of 1896, Hickory King corn grown from seed obtained in Illinois, was more productive than Hickory King corn grown from seed that had become acclimatized in Alabama. The results secured in our comparative test of fourteen northern and southern varieties, (page 364) are suggestive as showing the relatively heavy yields produced by northern seed corn.

LETTERS FROM CUSTOMERS.

Mr. J. Behm, Paris, Texas, writes:—"Your timely article in Farm and Ranch on the subject of the right kind of northern seed corn to beat hot winds and drouth with, agrees with my observations in the surrounding corn fields. And that is, that many who heretofore have not benefitted by growing corn from northern seed have had the wrong varieties. Now that we have the object lesson of last year's crop before us, nearly every farmer in this country will plant at least a portion of his crop with your seed corn. In fact some of those that planted your corn last year, notwithstanding they have what they raised on hand will buy your seed again this spring, preferring not to take chances."

Mr. C. F. Moore, Bryan, Texas, writes:—"As a general thing all the farmers near here who planted northern grown seed corn this year (1898) are well pleased with it. There is a growing demand for it here.

Mr. W. M. Alfred, Tyler, Texas, writes:—"I know from experience that the right kind of northern corn does extra well here for one or two years, or before it becomes acclimatized."

Mr. W. T. Langley, Camp Hill, Ala., writes:—"The corn I got from you last spring, did extremely well for me this year (1898). My son-in-law planted some of it after harvesting his oats and it yielded forty bushels per acre for him. My neighbors all want seed of it."

Mr. E. L. McAlexander, Mack, Miss., writes:—"The corn I got from you last spring (1898) yielded full fifty bushels per acre on very thin land. Or about twelve bushels per acre more than my other fine corn."

Mr. E. A. Murray, Columbus, Ga., writes:—"Both sorts of corn that I got from you last spring did exceedingly well for me. Making what is considered an extra good yield here."

Mr. J. A. Rymph, Harper, Kansas, writes:— 'The corn I got from you last spring will make double the yield per acre over Kansas native corn grown alongside. My neighbors want seed of it."

Mr. J. C. Lyon, Elmo, Texas, writes:—"You have the corn for this country to succeed every year in making a crop. But my experience teaches me that to get the best yields from it, it should be left growing fully twice as many stalks per hill as our native corn. And that it makes its best yield the first year of its growth here. Myself and many neighbors intend giving you a good order next spring (1899). Your corn makes much better ears than, and does not overshoot itself like the common run-out northern corn shipped here for feed.

Mr. J. A. Croom. Harmony, Ark., writes:—"The corn I got from you last spring (1898) was the best of eight varieties which I raised. It matured about thirty days before and yielded fully one-third more bushels per acre than our native corn,"

Mr. W. H. Crawford, Dickinson, Texas, writes:—"I have just read in today's (Jan. 30, 1898) issue of 'Farm and Ranch,' your article on thoroughbred Illinois seed corn, and my experience agrees with every word you say. One of my neighbors, who moved here from Illinois, gave me some seed corn which he brought with him. I obtained from it the best crop of corn I have ever grown."

Mr. F. M. Miller Eastland, Texas, writes:—"Where can I procure purely bred northern seed corn? I have made good corn from it here when my neighbors made almost a failure with our Texas native corn."

Jane R Mizell, Gibsland, La., writes:—"The corn I got from you last spring did splendidly for me. My neighbors are carried away with it, and say they must get seed of it next spring."

Thus the south makes abundant forage production possible in the north, with her nine months of necessary stock feeding. And the north reciprocates by making corn production possible in the south during droughty years.

We are accustomed to saying that nothing is impossible with God. But little has man hitherto known of the gigantic possibilities that lie hidden under some of His most natural laws, and of the mighty forces that are everywhere awaiting the quickening touch of human ingenuity.

To summarize I will again say that northern corn to be successfully grown in the south, must be of the latest thoroughbred sorts that can be well matured in the northern states. And as the stalks of our largest corn here grows so much smaller than the stalks of your native sorts, our northern corn can be planted two or three kernels per hill there, and bear its full sized ears. **Champion White Pearl, Champion Yellow Dent,** Golden Beauty, Hickory King, St. Charles White, Blount's Prolific, Dugan's White Prolific, Cuban Giant, Improved Leaming, and Improved Early Golden Dent (Buist's) are some of the best varieties for the southern states and Kansas. Reports from my customers confirm this.

RAPID TRANSIT.

I have rapid transit arrangements to many points. And with my system of tracing, I have greatly lessened delay in the transit of my shipment.

The past spring I succeeded in reaching most Texas points in seven to twelve days. Most Louisiana points in six to ten days, and most Georgia points in seven to twelve days. It is always important to you to get your seed through quickly. You may rest assured that I will always use every means in my power to hurry your seeds through. My southern trade has much more than quadrupled itself during the past three years. I have a large number of southern customers who are annually increasing their orders to me.

I will prepay freight charges on corn in lots of two bushels or more to all points in Texas, except points in extreme West Texas, for fifty-five cents per bushel, additional.

Trusting to be favored with your orders, which will be shipped quickly by fast freight, and urgently traced to rush through, and to hear from you often, I am in meantime

YOURS FOR GOOD FIELD SEEDS

J. C. SUFFERN.

VOORHIES, ILLINOIS, JANUARY 20, 1901.

| ORIGINATOR OF FIELD CORN. | Champion White Pearl. Champion Yellow Dent. | POP CORN. | Monarch White Rice. Red Beauty. Dye Cob Pop Corn. |

WHITE BEAUTY SUNFLOWER.

HOW TO GET YOUR SEED FREE.

Take this catalogue to all of your neighbors, and read to them the articles on pages 6, 7, 8, 9, and bottom of page 16. You will then be enabled to easily secure their order—at the prices we charge for the smaller quantities. You will then be entitled to our much lower prices on the larger quantities. Thus you will not only secure what seeds you want at no cost to you, but perhaps make some extra money besides. Your club order will not cost much if any more in freight charges, than would one-half or one bushel shipments. As larger quantities secure much lower freight rates. See bottom of page 2 of order sheet. We will label each lot in your club order with the name of the person for whom it is intended, and ship all in your name. Almost half of the orders we receive are club orders.

CHOICE FIELD CORN.

It has ever been my aim to raise and sell only the "tried and true" superior **high bred** kinds of field seeds. Which are great practical improvements over the old run out kinds. Being as much superior to them as thoroughbred cattle is to scrubs. And which yield much larger quantities of much better quality than old kinds. Thus producing large actual gains, in dollars and cents, to those who raise them. I raise no corn that has an ear at every joint, and a quart of shelled corn in the tassel. No potatoes that cover the ground when dug. No overbearing watermelon—gooseberries, etc. Many of the so-called "Wonderful" new kinds of corn, I have found to be merely old well known kinds, introduced under new names, and sold under inflated extravagant claims. I have one such in mind, that was so introduced. And instead of being a benefit to purchasers, it has been really a damage to thousands of farmers, in all parts of the country. I do not catalogue it. As I want nothing to do with such sorts. The kinds I offer for sale, must first have been tried in all parts of the country, before I will think of offering them for sale. It has also been my greatest care to accurately describe all the seeds I offer for sale. Just as I know them, from having raised them on my own seed farm.

I make a **SPECIALTY** of **SEED CORN.** Having spent many years in improving and perfecting the corn plant. (I am still at it.) During these years, I have originated a number of new varieties of Corn. Every one of which have stood the test of time and proven a great success in most parts of the country, have become recognized staples of the seed trade. One variety of which, particularly—Champion White Pearl, (to my positive knowledge there are several other kinds offered under its name.) I will venture to say: has benefitted the farmers of the United States, to the extent of over 100 millions of dollars, in increased yields, and fine quality, over what they would have realized with old kinds. (See testimonials on last page of cover.) As there are few townships in which it has not been raised, during the fourteen years since I introduced it. For my Champion **Yellow** Dent Corn, I predict as great a success all over the U. S., as my C. W. Pearl Corn has achieved, I can say truly, that I have never raised or seen any other kind of yellow corn that combines so many good points as the Champion Yellow Dent does.

I have this year, as I always do, given all my varieties of Corn very careful sprouting tests. And find that there are **VERY FEW** grains that do not show a strong healthy sprout. The State Experiment Station at Urbana, Ill., has tested my Corn. Write them about anything you wish to know. They will answer you promptly.

I will further say: that I have much the largest, soundest, heaviest stock of Seed Corn to offer this year, that I have ever had.

It is pure and true to name, and nicely prepared for my customers. I send it shelled mostly. As nearly all of my customers want it shelled. As they have less freight charges to pay. Still I have some customers who want theirs in the ear. And I am always glad to send it in the ear if wanted so. But we do not shell nubbins. rotten ears, tips and all, as I regret to say, some has been, which I have at times received from certain seed firms. I only use about half (the best half) of the total product of an acre for seed. The other half I sell to grain merchants. Truly I find my best advertisements in my customers fields. I have plenty of almost every kind I offer, to fill all the orders which I may receive this year.

Below I quote the language of a large practical Missouri farmer: "Although I plant generally, a number of varieties of corn, in order to test their value, I select for my main crop. two kinds. First a large late kind for my early planting (if it does not rain so that I cannot plant early), and an 85 or 90 day corn for my late spring planting or to plant late on overflowed land, or to plant my whole crop with, in a spring like the present one. Generally this early corn does not yield as well as the large kinds, but if we have a severe July and August drouth, as we often do, the early corn will not grow to stalk so much, ear better, and outstrip the large late corn in yield. I always keep an early corn on my farm for replanting or late planting." Sensible is he, say I. I have planted 90 day corn on wheat stubble, on July the 5th, and raised a good crop—about 45 bushels per acre. I always plant it twice as thick as large corn. As the stalks do not grow so large, but make their average sized ear.

TWO NEW CORNS.—I have 2 very valuable new varieties of corn, which after extensive tests in all parts of the country have proven to be real and valuable improvements over old varieties I have none of these two kinds for sale this spring. But expect to grow them in sufficiently large quantities the following year, to be able to supply a large demand for them.

To every person sending me an order for seed corn, accompanied by the cash, prior to March 20th, I will send a large package of either of these corns free, provided they request it when sending their order.

SAMPLES OF CORN. To intending purchasers, who will agree in their applications to show my samples, and this catalogue to their neighbors who want seed corn, and send me their addresses, I will gladly mail small samples of 2 to 6 kinds of seed corn, free.

MY PRICES. The seed dealer who imagines that prices alone, govern trade, is laboring under a great mistake. **Prices alone**, do govern trade with a certain class. A class who want everything at panic prices. And whom no amount of cutting in the world will satisfy.

I do not attempt to compete in price with growers who pay little or no attention to the quality and excellence of their stock seed. The roguing of their growing crops or the good preparation of seeds for their trade. My aim is not so much to offer "**cut to the bone**" prices, as to offer **best stock for the money.** In fixing my prices for the coming season, I have carefully considered everything relating thereto. And have placed my prices as low as high class seeds can be grown and sold at a profit. And low enough so corn growers everywhere can afford to order at least 10 bushels or more of seed. Especially when they consider a profit of $7 to $12 per acre in the increased yields and quality to be obtained by a judicious change of seed, in addition to selling seed to neighbors, at good prices. Figure on it for yourselves. My profit per bushel is not large, but my profit is in the large number of bushels sold. I have made my prices on a basis of the market price of No. 2 corn, No. 2 wheat, etc. in Chicago, and St. Louis, on Jan. 20, '98. Whether the markets decline, or advance, after this date, I will in either case send you your money's worth.

If other reliable dealers quote any of the same varieties of seed lower than I do, then clip their prices from their catalogue (and give me their name) and mail with your order. Upon receipt of which, and the cash, I will fill your order. But otherwise, any correspondence looking to a reduction of my prices, will prove futile. But lower prices will be allowed on larger quantities than 10 bushels.

Local dealers and others interested in having you buy at home constantly exaggerate the cost of shipping, to both your and our disadvantage. We will gladly quote both freight and express rates to your town upon request. **Freight and express rates have been much reduced.**

"*When a variety of seed is in the path of degeneracy, the best soil in the country, the most favorable season and the most thorough cultivation will fail to produce a satisfactory crop.*"

EDWARD TODD.

CHAMPION YELLOW DENT CORN.

A grand new Thoroughbred Corn. Tested and Proved. All and more than claimed for it — See Page 1. — INTRODUCED IN 1894.

Much encouraged by the success which the famous Champion White Pearl Corn (of which I am originator,) has achieved throughout the land, I have, during the past 10 years, been breeding up towards a high ideal, a main crop superior yellow dent corn, suitable for general and extensive culture in the corn states.

First by a combination of crosses of several leading standard yellow sorts.

Subsequently by a continuous systematic selection, grasping, accumulating, and perpetuating, the superior merits of its parents, and the good points which nature continually evolves. Constantly roguing out the undesirable points.

After the 12th generation, its type and characteristics are thoroughly fixed. And I now believe my former ideal almost fully realized. For in all my extensive experience as a corn grower, I have never seen a variety that combined so many superior points necessary to the making up of a first-class main crop yellow dent corn. In fact it is what they call an "all rounder." Superior in every point. It now stands alone in my estimation, as the fittest and most superior general crop yellow dent corn for extensive field culture in all localities south of the latitude of the northern boundary of Illinois.

It will undoubtedly become a very popular early yellow "crop corn" throughout the Cotton States. Where it fully makes its ear in July, before the usual August drouths begin. Making good yields when the late native sorts make almost nothing. A letter now before me, just received from a gentleman in Central Texas, who made a test of it there, last year, fully demonstrates this. See what he says under heading of testimonials, on 4th cover page. While critical tests throughout the corn states, prove that it is all, and more, than I claim for it. In my own locality, where it is the crowned King of yellow corn, it is grown almost to the exclusion of all other yellow sorts, for miles in every direction. And anything to find such general favor at home, must possess great merit. I do not claim for it, magical wonderful yields. But I do claim it to be a remarkably uniform large yielding sure crop sort. Eighty to 100 bushels per acre over large fields, with only ordinary cultivation is a common occurrence. And high average yields for a series of years, are what fatten the farmers "pocket books." Then it rarely fails to produce paying crops even in the most unfavorable seasons. Very diligent selection has produced a profuse growth of pollen in the tassel, and an abundance of silk on the ear. And the simultaneous appearance of these on the same stalk, and on all the individual stalks, combine to produce a very perfect fertilization. To this fact alone do I attribute its high average yields, and uniformly superior quality of grain.

As the originator of this corn, I desire that it make its way into general public favor solely by a reasonable extolling of its merits. And not meteoric like, to be sold under inflated extravagant claims.

It can be depended upon, when planted by June 15th, to make good corn by Sept. 15th. When planted early, matures in 100 days. The grain, owing to an unusually large solid oily germ, has peculiarly high germinating powers, seldom germinating less than 100 per cent. Truly a most valuable feature.

● It makes a rapid strong healthy spring growth. A short thick strong jointed stalk, with a profuse growth of air roots which hold it firm against storms. It has very long tap roots, which reach deep down after moisture during dry weather. A very profuse growth of pollen and silk, producing very long heavy well filled ears, which grow upon very short small shanks, close to and low upon the stalk, and contains 16 very straight compact rows of rich golden colored starchy oily grain of a uniformly high grade, and which makes a No. 1 feeding and milling corn. It has a very small red cob. Get a start of it now. It will make extra dollars for you in future years.

MY PRICES—By Freight or Express.—Peck 45c, ½ bus. 85c, one bus. $1.65. 2 bus. $3.10, 5 bus $7.40, 10 bus. $14.50. Postpaid prices—1 lb 40c, 3 lbs $1.00

A sample ear put in each bushel of shelled corn. I recommend C. Y. Dent for all points south of Northern Ohio, South Central Mich., Northern Ills., North Central Iowa, and North Central Neb.

I have plenty of it to fill all orders.

SEE ILLUSTRATION of C. Y. Dent on outside page of cover. It is an exact representation of an ear which I husked on Sept. 14, 1894.

Champion White Pearl.

The popular Dent Corn, which stands to-day without a peer. The most complete success of the age. Confirmations crowd in from the east, the west, the north, the south. The handsomest white dent corn ever seen. Very productive, ripens in 90 to 100 days. Brought to its present high standard by 21 years of continuous, systematic selection.

In the introduction and dissemination of this corn, my former claims (14 years ago), have been abundantly borne out. Instead of sinking into oblivion in two or three years, as do many high blown sorts, it has solely on its own merits, grown into such general public favor, that to-day it is recognized and catalogued as the leading standard variety of thoroughbred pure white medium sized early white dent-corn. It did not sprout up in a year or two, but I have brought it to its present high standard by 21 years continuous accumulative selection. Each year placing it on a still higher plane of purity, vigor and perfection. So that to-day it is far ahead of 14 years ago. It scored the highest average yield at the Illinois Agricultural Experiment Station, Urbana, Ill., during an extensive variety test, covering a period

ENGRAVED FROM A PHOTOGRAPH.

of 6 years, 1888 to 1893 inclusive. See bulletin 31, March, 1894. In 1893 it was far ahead of a number of varieties, at the Oklahoma Experiment Station, Stillwater, Okla. See bulletin 10, for 1893. In 1890 and again in in 1892, it took first premium at the Iowa State Fair, and went to Columbian Exposition as the best corn from Iowa. It has won first premium at Nebraska state fair for the period of 6 years. Indeed, its superiority is so well known, and so widespread, that nothing further need be said in its favor here. I recommend it for all localities south of Detroit, Mich., Southern Wisconsin, Northern Iowa, and Northern Nebraska.

True merit alone, has won bright laurels for this corn. It being now recognized as the leading standard sort of **pure** white, very long grained very starchy best milling early general crop corn of the highest possible quality. Very small white cob. Short thick robust deeply rooting stalk, with ear very low upon it. Thus standing severe storms and droughts well. Very uniform in fertilization and maturity. Maturing in 100 days. An immensely high average yielder all over the corn belt, and in the Cotton States. A beauty, and in every respect a first-class white sure cropping corn.

At my prices it will cost you only about 25c. per acre to plant your whole crop with the C. W. Pearl **Corn. And which is** only about half of what oats seeding costs. Then why plant poor run out corn. (In a **letter just received from** an old customer of mine—Mr. J. B. Piersol, of Rockwell P. O. in Northern Iowa, **he says**—"The corn I got from you last spring, yielded most 2 bushels of corn per acre. Which was better than our corn from other seed—see testimonials - I attribute the extra yield to the change of seed. Which I have found to be of great advantage.") I can assure you that one acre of it will yield more than enough extra for you, to pay for 3 to 5 bags of my seed.

MY PRICES—By mail postpaid. lb. 30c. 3 lbs. 75c. By express or freight, Peck 45c. ½ bus. 75c. One bus. $1.40. 2 bus. $2.55 5 bus. $6.00. 10 bus. $11.50. New extra heavy seamless bags in which to ship each 2 bus. or less of seed corn you order, I charge 15c. extra for. Do not fail to send their cost when you order. Write for my special prices on larger quantities than 10 bus. I ship by freight mostly, and trace well to hurry seed through.

SEE ILLUSTRATION of C. Y. Dent on outside page of cover. It is an exact representation of an ear which I husked on September 14, 1894. Being made by an engraver—Mr. A. Blanc, 314 N. 11th st.

IMPROVED LEAMING CORN (Medium Yellow Dent.)

This popular and distinct variety of yellow dent corn, certainly has beyond question, reached the grandest success of any yellow dent corn that has ever been brought before the farming public. It was brought to its present high state of perfection by 30 years continuous systematic selection. By its originator—J. S. Leaming, of Clinton Co., Ohio. This noted and much praised corn, was first brought to popular public notice at the World's Exposition, Paris, France, in 1873, where it received the highest award for a yellow field corn. Since then it has been tested all over the United States and has given fine satisfaction. This is a medium-sized, golden yellow corn. The stalks grow to a medium height, not large, but thick, has but few suckers, and often produce two fine ears, which in the true Leaming, are low upon the stalk. The grain is long, narrow, and thick, and sets very close together in the rows. The cob is medium-sized and very red. This corn husks and shells very easily, and weighs 60 to 62 pounds per measured bushel, and matures in 90 to 100 days. **Don't fail to try this Grand Corn.** My seed was grown from seed obtained direct from the originator, and is pure. I recommend this corn for all localities South of Chicago, Ill., Toledo, Ohio, and Omaha, Neb. **Prices:** By mail postpaid, Lb. 25c. 3 lbs. 70c. By express or freight, Peck 40c. ½ bus. 70c. One bus. $1.35. 2 bus. $2.45. 5 bus. $5.75. 10 bus. $11.00. Write for my special prices on larger quantities than 10 bus. See freight rates, on page 5.

HICKORY KING CORN (Medium White Dent.)

This new white field corn has *the largest grains*, with *the smallest cob* of any white corn ever introduced. So large are the grains, and so extremely small the cob that on an ear broken in half *a single grain will almost completely cover the cob.* No other variety of field corn that I have ever seen will do this. Of strong, vigorous growth, the stalks take a firm hold in the ground and stand upright, resisting the severest storms, the stalks generally bear two ears, and occasionally three. It yields splendid crops on light soil, and is undoubtedly a more productive white corn to bulk of ears than any other variety. It makes a splendid quality of corn meal and is "just the thing" for cattle feeding. As it is almost all corn, with but very little cob. I recommend it for all localities south of Central Ohio, Central Illinois, and Northern Kansas. It matures in 115 to 125 days. PRICES: Same as for **Improved Leaming Corn.**

DUNGAN'S WHITE PROLIFIC CORN (A Large White Dent.)

This large white dent corn was introduced by Mr. S. W. Dungan, of Indiana. It has a large amount of foliage, and stands drouth better than some kinds. It is much like my C. W. Pearl Corn, and much the same description will answer for it, except that it is not so early. My stock was grown from seed grown from headquarters stock. And is pure and true. I recommend it for about same latitude north as Golden Beauty. **PRICES:** Same as for Improved Leaming **Corn.**

BLOUNT'S WHITE PROLIFIC CORN (Or Mammoth Ensilage.)

This excellent variety of fodder corn, was originated by O. E. Blount, now of Colorado Agric. Experiment Station. It has produced over 40 tons of green fodder per acre. And in 1889, on my seed farm, it produced 118 bushels of grain per acre. The ears are long, slender, and average 2 per stalk. I have seen 8 ears of it on one stalk. It matures in about 125 days. I recommend it for all localities south of Central Ohio, Central Illinois, and Northern Kansas, for grain and north indefinitely for fodder.

CUBAN GIANT CORN (Or White Cob Ensilage.)

This is much similar to the well known St. Charles White. But has a white cob, longer and slimmer ear, and matures about 15 days earlier. It is a large fodder yielder, and a very heavy grain yielder. In fact an all round good white dent corn, and does extra well in the Cotton states. PRICES: Same as for **Improved Leaming Corn.**

ST. CHARLES WHITE CORN (A Large White Dent.)

A large growing red cobbed white dent corn, with a profuse growth of foliage. Originated and much esteemed in the vicinity of St. Louis, Mo., as a general crop sort. And quite popular in the north as an Ensilage corn. I have nice pure seed. It will mature wherever **Golden Beauty Corn** will. **PRICES: Same as for Improved Leaming Corn.**

GOLDEN BEAUTY CORN (A Large Yellow Dent.)

I have never seen a more handsome yellow dent corn than this. It has nicely shaped ears, well filled out, and containing about 16 rows of golden yellow-colored, long, broad grains. It is a very heavy yielder. And the fact that it has a medium soft grain, makes it valuable for stock feeding. I highly recommend this corn, for all points south of Columbus, O., Springfield, Ill., or Atchison, Kan. The stalk is strong, and medium tall. It matures in 110 days. **PRICES:** Same as for **Improved Leaming.**

EARLY BUTLER CORN (90 Day Yellow Dent.)

This new Early Dent Corn was first sent out three years ago and has grown in popularity very fast. It has the largest ear of any of the first very early dent corns. Also the deepest grain and the most rows on the cob. It grows strong, rank and quick, and will out sell any early variety in cultivation. On trial one bushel of seventy pounds shelled sixty-four and one-half pounds, leaving only five and one-half pounds of cobs. Every farmer should give this fine yellow corn a trial. **PRICES:** Same as for **Champion White Pearl Corn.** It will do well wherever the Pride of the North will, but is a larger corn.

Don't forget to ask your neighbor to join you in sending for some of our good varieties of corn.

WHITE CAP YELLOW DENT CORN

This corn comes from a large grower of all kinds of seed corn, and is a corn of great merit. It grows large ears and matures early. The ear grows almost as large as Leaming and is from seven to ten days earlier, and on poor, thin soil will yield thirty per cent more corn. It grows strong, rank and quick, and, it is claimed, will produce more corn on poor, thin soils than any other kind now in cultivation. It will be appreciated by those living in droughty sections and by those farmers who have poor, thin soil, while on strong, rich soil it has no superior. The tip end of the grains are white, the inside yellow, making it a beautiful color. Large growers in the corn belt, as well as those out of it, will be pleased with this corn. **Price:** Same as for Champion White Pearl Corn.

PRIDE OF THE NORTH CORN.

This is one of the earliest dent corns in cultivation. When planted in Illinois, on the 4th of July, it has fully matured before frost; it can be planted twice as thick in the hill as large corn, and at the same time bear a full sized ear; this is a small sized dent corn and matures in 87 days. The stalk is short and thick, and stands storms well. Ear is from 7 to 10 inches in length, and 1¾ inches in diameter; the grain is of a deep yellow color, is long, thick and narrow, and of a very oily nature; the cob is very small and red. I highly recommend it for all localities south of Central Mich., Central Minn., and Central Dak. See testimonials on page 16. **PRICES:** Same as for **Champion White Pearl Corn.**

SILVER WHITE LINT CORN (A Fine Hominy Corn)

This popular thorough-bred large white flint corn, originated in New York. Its ears often grow 15 inches long, and produce 50 to 60 bushels per acre. It is a very fine hominy corn. It is also fine for early fall hog feed. It matures in about 85 days. **Prices:** Same as for C. W. Pearl Corn.

I Guarantee Safe arrival of the seed at your station. Do not fail to remit for sacks, 15c each.

In your orders please state 2d choice, in case I am out of your 1st choice.

IOWA GOLD MINE CORN (An Early Yellow Dent.)

A very popular yellow dent corn originated in Central Iowa. It has a very long yellow grain, and very small red cob. By a careful test, 400 measured bushels of its ears shelled out 456 bus. It matures in about 95 days. And gives good satisfaction as far north as northern Iowa. My seed was grown from direct headquarters stock. Price: Same as for Champion White Pearl Corn.

IOWA SILVER MINE CORN.

A new early white dent corn introduced from Iowa last spring. It is a 95 day good yielding, pure white corn. From records in various parts of the corn belt, it has given good satisfaction. My stock seed was purchased from the introducers.

PRICES: Same as for **Champion White Pearl.**

I desire all my readers to write me their experience—their opinions on novelties. How they manage. What new ideas they have. What fine varieties of wheat, oats, corn, or potatoes have you this year? Which kinds have done the best for you? Where did you get your start of them.

Mr. Henry Brown, Crab Orchard, P. O. in N. W, Missouri, says: "The C. W. Pearl corn I got from you, I planted last and gathered first. It yielded 60 bushels per acre. It is the purest, whitest and best bread corn I ever saw; neighbors think very highly of it.

Mr. J. A. Titus, Lawn Ridge, Marshall Co., Ill., says: "I had good success with the seed oats which I bought from you. They yielded 16 bushels per acre more than other oats I raised on same kind of ground and same kind of cultivation.

CHOICE SWEET CORN.

Stowell's Evergreen. A late variety of excellent quality, remaining longer in green state than any other kinds.

Gold Coin. This is 10 days earlier than Stowell's Evergreen, similar in appearance except kernels are yellow; very productive. two or three ears on a stalk; very sweet.

Egyptian. Ears large. Ripening late. Sweet; prolific; demands a high price in market.

Country Gentleman. This distinct, medium-late popular variety, has the smallest cob, and deepest grain of any known variety. The kernel is white, tender and juicy. It is very productive.

None Such. A new second early sort, of great merit. The originator (in northern Ohio) offers $100, for its equal in quality. It has a pink cob and white grain. Good sized ears, and is a big yielder. I have the genuine seed.

PRICES: Postpaid, packet 5c. qt. 30c. By Express or fast freight Peck $1.00. Bush. $3.00, for all of above kinds of sweet corn.

MY POP CORN SEED.

The growing of pop corn, the last few years has become quite an industry And the country has been greatly in need of pure uniform varieties. As you will note below, I offer seed of popular varieties. I take extra care to grow very pure seed, and to prepare it nicely—shelled and re-cleaned. I can also furnish selected ears at same prices as the shelled corn. The past year my trade on pop corn seed, more than quadrupled over the previous year.

NEW RED BEAUTY.

This valuable new rice pop corn was originated by an expert pop corn grower of Illinois, who while rogueing a field of Snow Ball pop corn, in the summer of 1888, discovered a sport of a remarkably peculiar style. Since, by isolation and careful accumulative selection he has secured a variety, which for rare beauty, extreme earliness, great productiveness, crispness, tenderness, great depth of grain, and smallness of cob cannot be equaled. 50 bushels per acre being a common yield. It pops splendidly 4 months from time it is planted. In every respect a first-class family pop corn.

PRICES for Red Beauty; postpaid, packet, 10c: one ℔ 40c. By express or freight, Peck $2.00. One bushel (60 ℔s. shelled) $7.00.

MONARCH WHITE RICE.

After 10 years very careful systematic selection I have succeeded in breeding up a variety of pop corn which combines the most desirable qualities, viz: great productiveness, early maturity, tenderness, sweetness, beautiful snow white color, greatest bulk after being parched, uniformity of type, and the fact that its thorn at outer end of grain, turns toward the cob, forming a hook, which does not prick the hands when husking. Thus avoiding the common objection to growing rice pop corn. This variety parches well by December 1st, of the year in which it is grown. And in time for the holiday trade. Whereas most varieties must be carried over into the next summer, before they are suitable to the parching trade. To which the **Monarch White Rice** sells for a higher price than any other sort. It bears from 2 to 6 ears per stalk, weighs 36 ℔s. per bushel of ears when dry, and produces 1500 to 2000 ℔s. per acre. Like C. W. P. Corn, this practical, early pop corn is steadily growing into general favor. It has "come to stay." If you miss it, you will miss a good thing.

PRICES: Postpaid, packet 10c. Lb. 35c. 3 ℔s. 90c. By Express or fast freight, Peck $1.75 One bus. (60 ℔s. shelled) $6.00.

Prices, post paid for these 8 sorts..
{ Silver Lace..........
Queens Golden......
Mapledale Prolific..
Ills. Snow Ball......
Mammoth Rice ......
New Red Rice.......
Page's Striped Rice.
Tattooed Yankee. }
packet 10c
pound 25c
3 ℔s. 65c

By Express or freight { Peck, shelled, ...$1.60
1 bushel. (60 ℔ shelled... 5.25 }

CHICE SEED OATS.

White Bonanza Oats.—This is the variety that was awarded the American Agriculturists' special $500 prize, for a yield in Orleans Co., New York, of over 133 bus. per acre, in 1889. It is an extra nice, heavy white oats. I highly recommend it.

Clydesdale or *Race Horse Oats*—A very early variety, weighing 45 ℔s, and over per measured bushel. Well-cleaned samples have weighed over 50 ℔s The straw is straight and stiff, holding up well its immense branching heads, 20 inches in length, with rather short plump grains. It is reported as having yielded from 90 to 100 bushels per acre.

LINCOLN OATS.—This valuable new white oats, first introduced in 1893, has been largely sold in all sections of the country, and has given fine satisfaction. My seed was grown from stock obtained direct from the introducers last spring.

MEXICAN GRAY OATS.—A new extra early gray oats, particularly suited to the south and west. As it is so early that it matures its grain before hot winds or rust set in. Straw short and thick. A big yielder everywhere almost.

TEXAS RED RUST PROOF OATS.—At the Illinois Experiment Station, Urbana, Ills.; this new red oats has proved to be the largest yielder of many varieties there. It does well on black soils throughout the north. It is very early.

My Prices.—For any of the above named kinds of oats are as follows: Postpaid, 1-lb. 25c 3-lbs. 60c. By express or fast freight, Peck 30c. ¼-bus. 50c. O e bus. 85c. 2 bus. $1.60. 5 bus. $3.50. 10 bus. $6.50.

CHOICE SEED POTATOES.

Potatoes will be shipped in favorable weather only. We commence shipping Potatoes about the first week in March. If you want your Potatoes shipped before March, please state so in your order. But we will not be responsible for damage they may sustain during transit from either cold or heat.

EARLY VARIETIES.

Early Six Weeks Market.—Ready for market in 6 weeks, matures in 75 days. It grows medium to large. Light flesh colored. Smooth. Eyes even with surface. They are so early that potato bugs have but little chance at them. They are solid and mealy, and are not excelled as a table potato.

The Crown Jewel.—New; a self-seedling of the Early Ohio; is about a week earlier than the Early Rose or Early Ohio, and will yield nearly double of either; quality the best. The Crown Jewel is a strikingly beautiful potato; shape oblong, size large, skin white and smooth, flesh pure white and floury, in keeping qualities is equal to the best.

Early Beauty of Hebron.—Extra Early, Resembles Early Rose, but matures a week earlier; grows very rapidly, which helps it withstand the attacks of insects. Skin smooth, white, sometimes pinkish tinted, but becomes white in Winter; tubers of good size, round, flat oblong in form; flesh white, solid and of delicate flavor.

LATE POTATOES.

Burpee's Superior.—Long, round or slightly flattened, skin pure white, netted; eyes plenty, rather small and even with the surface, giving it a very smooth, handsome appearance, size medium to large. vines large and vigorous, This is far ahead of Star and Burbank in all desirable qualities.

Rural New Yorker No. 2.—This new potato, introduced in 1889, is proving to be one of superior excellence. Oblong, round or oval; skin pure white, netted; eyes few and even with the surface; size large to very large, vines thrifty and strong. In productiveness and quality it is scarcely equaled. Remarkably vigorous, very productive.

EARLY PURITAN. This variety was originated by Mr. Coy of New York state, who originated the Beauty of Hebron and over a dozen other varieties. The skin and flesh are very white. It cooks dry and floury. *Its greatest value is in productiveness.* It yields nearly double that of the Early Rose; is early as Early Rose, and wonderfully dry when but half grown. The vines are vigorous and upright.

NEW QUEEN. Whether on poor thin soil or rich bottom land this potato has done surprisingly well. Very early, extra quality, wonderfully productive, size large, color white, shape long, smooth and clean. A fancy market variety.

PRICES for all above named varieties of potatoes are as follows—By Express or Fast Freight. One bushel, $1.65. One barrel 2¾ bushels, $4.00. **Prices subject to Changes of the Market.**

TUBEROUS ROOTED ARTICHOKES

In the writers' experience (also supported by many late writers' on the subject) much the greater part of hog sickness (mostly termed cholera) throughout the country, is directly due to diseases which have their origin in indigestion, caused by hogs not receiving a well balanced diet— too much corn and not enough muscle, tendon and bone forming food. A recent writer in the Tennesse Farmer, says: "I would prefer the product grown from one bushel of tame artichokes, as a digestion regulator, and disease preventative, to all the hog cholera cures obtainable." After eight years practical field experience with "tame" artichokes, I have concluded that when fed in connection with corn tame artichoke tubers (the wild artichoke is merely a pest, difficult to eradicate) are by far, and all odds the healthiest, handiest and cheapest hog food than can be grown. They are just as valuable as a digestion regulator and cheap food for horses, cattle and sheep. On ground that will produce fifty bushels of corn per acre, 500 to 1000 bushels of them can easily be grown. The writer easily eradicates a patch of tame artichokes by sowing to oats, or plowing under the young plants when they are about eighteen inches high. April is the best spring month in which to plant them. Five bushels of cut tubers per acre. If our stock of tubers is exhausted when your order arrives, we will book it, and ship in October 1899. Full directions for planting, cultivating, etc., will be sent with each order.

MAMMOTH WHITE FRENCH This fine variety was recently brought from France. Where it is largely used for human food as well as for stock feed. It grows larger and nearer the surface, and is better for pickling than other sorts.

WHITE JERUSALEM The peculiarity of this sort is its predominance of pinkish eyes. It also grows more in clusters than other sorts. It makes enormous yields, One acre being worth about ten acres of corn for hogs.

PRICES For each of these two kinds of artichokes are: Postpaid, 1b. 25c. By express or fast freight, Peck 40c. ½ bu. 75c. One bushel $1.10 5-bu. $4.75. I ship in sacks.

MISCELLANEOUS FARM SEEDS.

FIELD PEAS.

CANADIAN FIELD PEAS. Valuable for Northern climates for cattle feeding. Used as feed for pigeons, etc., and for green soiling. Pk., 50c; bu., $1.75.

CLAY COLORED. Pk., 50c; bu., $1.75.

SOUTHERN BLACKEYE COW. Also known as Sand Pea, a small white variety with black eye. Sow two bushels to the acre. Peck, 60c; bu., $2.00.

WHIP-POOR-WILL. Peck, 60c; bu., $2.00.

SPRING VETCHES, or TARES. Pk., $1.50; bu. (60 lbs.), $4.50.

White Beauty Sunflower.

For eight years I have been breeding towards a pure white Mammoth Sunflower. A very difficult, patient undertaking it has been. But now I can exclaim: **EUREKA! I have it at last.** A sunflower with Snow White Seeds. **It's a novelty indeed. A novelty in 1,000.** And is sure to meet with a large and enduring sale.

After years of careful selection I am rewarded with a purely bred Mammoth Single-head Sunflower with pure snow white seeds, which on account of the deficiency of strong coloring matter in the outer covering of their kernels, are much superior to the darker sorts for stock and poultry food. It also produces a much milder, better flavored oil.

This strikingly distinct new sort, is not only the most beautiful, the most vigorous, the most valuable for stock and poultry feeding, and for oil production, but owing to the fact that all its powers are expended in producing one mammoth head, it is simply a marvel for productiveness. Out-yielding the old sorts almost two to one. 3000 lbs. per acre being no unusual yield. I feel much gratified in being able to offer it to the trade. Being confident that it will take the lead in Sunflower production. **Price.**—Packet 10 cts., ½-lb. 35 cts.; lb 65 cts.; 2 lbs. $1.00, postpaid.

Money Insured.—I guarantee to hold myself responsible for the safe arrival of all remittances, when sent according to my instructions.

Mammoth Russian Sunflower.—A standard well known gray seeded variety. Large packet 10 c.; 1 lb. 25c postpaid.

→New customers are requested to investigate my standing.

Errors will occur in spite of us—no one is infallible. You will find me ready to do the right thing in case of an error.

Freight Rates are as low, and in many cases lower, to points in Ohio, Tenn., and distant states, than to points in Illinois. See table of rates on page 5.

MY 1902 CATALOGUE

will be ready about January 20, 1902. If from any cause you fail to receive a copy of it before March 15, you can order from this catalogue, as prices will be about the same. In every case, we will send your money's worth or abide by instructions you give when you send your order. It is always my aim to make your dealings with me pay you. For only by so doing can I expect your continued patronage and that of your friends.

SWEET POTATO PUMPKIN. - This is the best variety for making pies and custards, that I ever saw. When baked it is much superior to sweet potatoes. Flesh creamy white, very fine grained, dry and brittle. It grows to medium size, is very prolific, and keeps well until late in the spring. PRICES—Large packet 10c. ¼-lb. 45c. Lb. $1.40 postpaid.

WEED SEEDS.—In nothing about my business am I more careful, than in keeping all dangerous weed seeds, such as Canada thistle, wheat thief, cockle, etc., out of my seed grain. I have at times received from eastern seedsmen, seed grain that was full of these noxious weed seeds. Seeds which I each year plant on my own farm, from which I grow my large seed crops, are grown from very carefully hand-picked seed. All noxious weeds, impure grain, etc., being picked out. I let no seed grain leave my establishment which contain these foul weed seeds, if I know it. Be careful of whom you purchase.

SUBSTITUTING.—Orders received before Mch. 20, will be filled without substituting, unless permission is given to substitute. After March 20, as there will be no time for correspondence, we reserve the right to fill any order, if necessary, with other varieties equally good and of the same season, unless the order distinctly states "No Substitution Allowed."

SNOW WHITE DENT CORN

THE GRANDEST MILLING CORN IN THE WORLD.

Today there are more than thirty commercial articles made from white corn. The food products, especially, have come rapidly to the front during the past few years. And the business of manufacturing white corn goods promises enormous expansion prior to the year 1910.

But millers have been greatly hampered by the poor, unfitted quality of the white corn that has heretofore been grown. The ordinary white corn of the great corn belt is of a dull straw colored white shade, with a liberal admixture of yellow, red, striped, blue, and unsound small sized grains, and falls far short of meeting millers' requirements for making the desired quality of brewer's grits, meal, hominy, etc. In order to economically manufacture corn goods of the desired quality and whiteness, millers require large, hard, smooth kerneled, very white grained corn.

Much of the ordinary white corn of the country is so late in its maturing season that it cannot be depended upon to produce a uniformly high grade of milling corn during a series of years, even if it were pure and white enough in color. Happily, I have bred "Snow White Dent Corn" to the point where it combines extremely pure, and very white color, with large size, compactness, and smoothness of grain, with sure maturity at any point south of the 43d parallel of latitude. So that it now is by all odds the grandest milling corn in the world. An extensive manufacturer of white corn goods, who uses 3500 bushels of corn daily, recently told me that if I would breed up such a corn as I personally know "Snow White Dent" to be, that he would give me an order for two or three cars of it, to place with farmers for seed, at his many grain buying stations. But I did not tell him that I had already bred such a corn, as I had contracted my crop of it to Mr. Wm. Henry Maule, the very reliable and noted Philadelphia seedsman, to whom all orders should be sent. His prices are as follows: 8 lbs., enough to plant one acre, three grains per hill, in rows three and one-half feet apart each way, sent by mail or express, prepaid, for $2.00; 1 lb., postpaid, 50c.; 3 lbs., $1 10. By express or freight, at purchaser's expense: one-fourth bus., $1.75; one-half bus., $3.00; one bus., $5.00. Not more than one bushel will be sold to any single person or firm. Send orders for seed of "Snow White Dent" direct to

WM. HENRY MAULE,

1711 FILBERT STREET.   PHILADELPHIA, PA.

DWARF ESSEX RAPE.

There are millions of acres of good land that lie idle part or all of the year to run to weeds, that can be sowed to this rape and produce the finest feed imaginable. It can be sown from May to September in this latitude. It can follow any other crop and furnishes most nutritious pasture. It is particularly valuable for sheep, being twice as nutritious as red clover. It is hardy in winter, resists severe droughts; in fact, of untold value. Sow 5 lbs. per acre broadcast; 3 lbs. per acre if drilled. By mail, pkt. 10c, lb. 35c, 3 lbs. $1. By frt. or ex., per lb. 15c, 100 lbs. $9.00.

BRED BROOM CORN SEED.

The unusually high prices which have prevailed for broom corn during the past three years (an average of more than $100 per ton), indicates clearly enough that demand has overtaken supply. In but few and restricted localities throughout the United States is broom corn grown on a commercial scale. Consequently there are but few farmers other than those in a few important broom corn belts who understand which are the most profitable varieties to grow, where best to procure good seed, or how best to prepare the land, plant, cultivate, harvest, cure, bale and market the crop in such a manner as to successfully compete with experienced growers in the old established broom corn belts, such as the writer is a resident of. There is at present a widespread and extensive inquiry from contemplative growers throughout the states for such information.

I have prepared a 1,500 word treatise on the subject, from A to Z, and will, upon request, mail a copy of same to all who purchase broom corn seed from me. Having lived in the great "Illinois Central" broom corn belt (which is more than 40 miles square), during the past 29 years, and having during the past 16 years grown and handled broom corn brush and its seed in a commercial way, with the latest improved machinery, I am thus in a position to supply practical working information. The all-important question with farmers who contemplate the growing of broom corn on a large scale is to provide themselves with "good seed," as the foundation for a good stand of growing plants which will, from the force of their accumulated good breeding, produce a high quality of "standard" high-priced brush. This most amateur growers fail to do. Their principal cause of failure being the unreliable, lowly-bred seed usually sold by some seed houses. Experienced growers of the great Illinois "Central" broom corn belt are prejudiced against the broom corn seed usually offered by seedsmen. To quote their words: "I would not plant it as a gift." Also quoting the words of one of the largest broom corn brokers in "Central": "There is a lot of stuff being offered throughout the United States called broom corn seed. Such stuff is liable to produce almost anything, provided it germinates, which is very doubtful." Living, as I do, in the 'Central" belt, with long experience in the business, I am in position to supply vital seed, which, from its careful breeding, produces "standard" high-priced brush.

I have learned that by far the most important question connected with broom corn growing is the securing of a good stand of growing plants, from "good seed." And "good seed" is that which has been carefully rogued while growing, being bred to the point where it produces bright green fine fibre brush (not red tipped), and whose heads produce a minimum amount of center stems, and do not crinkle at the stem end of head. "Good seed" is also very vital, from having been properly put through the "sweat" after being thrashed.

I have such seed to offer, and solicit orders for same.

Improved Evergreen Broom Corn.

This variety is an improvement on the usual evergreen broom corn varieties, inasmuch as it is about ten days earlier than the Tennessee Evergreen or Missouri Evergreen. Its brush is longer and stiffer, and is best for the manufacture of warehouse and long brooms. It yields on good corn land 600 to 800 pounds of brush per acre. It can be planted to good advantage on wheat or rye stubble. Seed light red color.

Tennessee Evergreen Broom Corn.

This noted variety of tall-growing Evergreen broom corn has been so thoroughly acclimatized in the great Illinois "Central" broom corn belt (which is more than 40 miles square), that it is the standby for the production of "standard" self-working brush. Owing to its seed being of a light golden color, it produces far greener, finer fibre brush than other Evergreen sorts. The great bulk of "standard" brush is grown from this sort.

California Golden Broom Corn.

This is an excellent standard sort of the Evergreen type. Seed is light red. It produces long brush, very free from the objectionable center stems. It is about one week earlier than the Tennessee Evergreen.

PRICES for all three varieties.

Pound, postpaid: 35c. By express or fast freight: Peck, 50c; half bushel, 95c; one bushel, $1.65; five bushels, $7.50; ten bushels, $14.50. One bushel will properly plant 16 acres.

Soja Bean or Coffee Bean.

The plant grows erect, 4½ feet high, with numerous branches covered with heavy foliage. The branches and stem are thickly set with clusters of pods, 2 beans in a pod. This seed has been sold under the name German Coffee Berry at extravagant prices. When roasted, ground and used as coffee it resembles the genuine article quite closely. Its value to farmers is in the ground beans, which make a very rich feed for milch cattle and also for other stock; also valuable as a fertilizer. Sow ½ bu. per acre broadcast or in drills 3 ft. apart; 12 in. between plants. By mail, pkt. 10c., pt. 20c., qt. 35c. By freight or express, ¼ bu. $1.00, bu. $3.50.

SUGAR CANE.

Early Amber Cane.—This popular and well known variety is the earliest, and makes the finest quality of amber syrup and good sugar. Succeeds well from Texas to Minnesota.

Early Orange Cane.—This is the favorite variety for molasses, from about the 38th degree of latitude, on south. It is about 12 days later than the Early Amber.

PRICES.—Postpaid of both kinds cane seed Lb. 25c. 3 lbs. 65c. By express or fast freight. Peck 60c. ¼-bu. $1.15. One bu. $2.25.

CLOVER-GRASS MIXTURES FOR PERMANENT PASTURES, MEADOWS OR PARTICULAR PURPOSES.

These Clover-Grass Mixtures are selected with the greatest of care and composed of such varieties as are best adapted for different varieties of soil and various purposes. From our own experience as well as from the experience gained by corresponding with our customers in every part of the country we are enabled to select in these Clover-Grass Mixtures not only the varieties as are suited to the soil but have them in the right proportion in each mixture. In every instance we mention the quantities which we recommend to be sown per acre; and not only have these proven to be sufficient in our own experiments carried on during several years, but they have proven to be equally successful and sufficient with our patrons, and there appears to be no need of sowing double the quantity as recommended by dealers in seeds. For dry ground we use a few pounds more per acre than for moist or rich ground, and for pastures we also use a few pounds more per acre than we recommend for meadows.

Quite often we are requested to quote the price of our Clover-Grass Mixtures in **bushel quantities**. We wish to state here that as long as we state the quantities needed per acre, customers can order from this whatever quantity is required to seed a certain piece. When customers wish or insist to buy these Clover-Grass Mixtures by bushels we will gladly quote the bushel price, which is based on 14 lbs to the bushel.

A.—CLOVER-GRASS MIXTURES FOR PERMANENT MEADOWS.

No. 1. For dry and high ground, light soils:

Red Fescue
Crested Dogstail
Hard Fescue
English Rye Grass
Sweet Vernal
Red Clover
Lucerne

Per Acre
20 lbs. @ 8c $1.60

50 lbs 3.90
100 lbs 7.50

No. 2 For dry and high ground, heavy or strong soils:

Tall Meadow Oat
Hard Fescue
English Rye Grass
Meadow Fescue
Red Top Grass
Sweet Vernal
Timothy
Red Clover
Alsyke Clover

Per Acre
20 lbs. @ 8c $1.60

50 lbs 3.90
100 lbs 7.50

No. 3. For moist ground and rich soils:

Meadow Foxtail
Meadow Fescue
Tall Meadow Oats
Italian Rye Grass
Timothy
Sweet Vernal
Alskye Clover

Per Acre
18 lbs. @ 9c $1.62

50 lbs 4.40
100 lbs 8.50

No. 4. For moist ground which is overflowed occasionally:

Tall Fescue
Meadow Fescue
Red Top Grass
Meadow Foxtail
Timothy
Alsyke Clover

Per Acre
16 lb. @ 9c $1.44

50 lbs 4 40
100 lbs 8 50

No. 5. For top seeding on marshes and swamps occasionally overflowed, the following mixture is especially adapted:

Water Spear Grass
Floating Meadow Grass
Red Top Grass
Tall Fescue Grass
Meadow Foxtail

Per Acre
10 lbs. @ 11c $1.10

50 lbs 5.35
100 lbs 10.50

B—CLOVER-GRASS MIXTURES FOR PERMANENT PASTURES

No. 1. For high and dry ground, light soils.

Hard Fescue
Red Fescue
Red Top Grass
Orchard Grass
English Rye Grass
Crested Dogstail
Yellow Oat Grass
Lucerne
Red Clover
White Clover

Per Acre
22 lbs. @ 8c $1.76

50 lbs 3.90
100 lbs 7.50

No. 2. For high and dry ground, heavy or clay soils:

Orchard Grass
English Rye Grass
Tall Meadow Oat
Blue Grass
Italian Rye Grass
Timothy
Red Fescue
Alsyke Clover
Red Clover
White Clover

Per Acre
22 lbs. @ 8c $1.76

50 lbs 3.90
100 lbs 7.50

No. 3. For moist ground and rich soils:

Meadow Foxtail
Blue Grass
Fowl Meadow
Creeping Bent Grass
Orchard Grass
English Rye Grass
Italian Rye Grass
Timothy
Red Top Grass
Red Clover
Alsyke Clover
White Clover

Per Acre
20 lbs. @ 9c $1.80

50 lbs 4.40
100 lbs 8.50

No. 4. For top seeding to improve a pasture on low rich ground or marshes:

Fowl Meadow
Creeping Bent
Red Top Grass
Tall Fescue
Alsyke Clover

Per Acre
10 lbs. @ 11c $1.10

50 lbs 5.35
100 lbs 10.50

LATEST AND BEST
SEED WHEAT
Tried and True, Hardy, Prolific Varieties.

As every farmer knows, we have been much in need of **Sure Crop, Stiff Strawed, Firm Chaff, Good Milling, Early Hardy Varieties of Wheat.** That would go through repeated freezing and thawing unhurt, yield full crops of extra quality, and sell at top prices. It is largely to your interest to grow the **hardy, prolific, good milling wheats.** How many farmers in your locality grow such wheat? Are they not in the habit of clinging to the old run out, unproductive sorts? You perhaps know of farmers who are an exception to this. They have been changing their seed. And are perhaps ready to do so again. Who if you will call their attention to it, will be anxious to help form a club for new seed wheat, this fall. I received one such club order for $276.00. See next page.

Mr. C. A. Pillsbury, of Minneapolis, Minn., the most extensive miller in the world, recently said: "I do not think the wheat situation warrants any foreboding of evil. In this country, consumption of wheat is increasing about 8 million to 10 million bushels annually against a decreasing supply. In the next 5 years the great mills in Minneapolis, will grind more wheat at over $1 per bushel, than under that price.

According to a table published by the **Chicago Board of Trade,** the average price of wheat for the past 32 years, has been over $1.10 per bushel. And for past 6 years, 82¾c per bu. It pays big to get your seed from a distant locality. Even if it is but the same variety you have been raising.

EARLY RED CLAUSON WHEAT.
The champion for black soil.

This productive and desirable brown chaff beardless, club-headed sort is destined to become a general favorite with all growers, as soon as known. Originated in that famous wheat district Genesee county, N. Y., where the great bulk of American wheat was grown before the west was opened up for cultivation. This originated from the popular Golden Cross the compact head, dark red grain, extreme hardness, rapid growth, and strong straw; and from the Clauson, baldness and red chaff, with very large kernels. **It is the earliest variety of winter wheat in existence.** Why run the risk of storms, excessive heat, insects and rust that are so apt to injure or destroy your wheat crop just as you feel that it is secure? **The Early Red Clauson** reduces the chances by coming in a week ahead of any other sort.

After 4 years rigid testing in all parts of the country, I highly recommend this valuable new wheat for all black or rich lands, where wheat is liable to lodge. It produced, the past season, on many large fields, on nearly all varieties of soil, from 40 to 50 bushels to the acre, and on some small fields more than this. Sow one bu. per acre. **Prices:** 1 bu. $1.85; 1 bag, 2¼ bu. $4.25; 5 bus. $8.25; 10 bus. $16. Write for prices on larger quantities.

These wheat prices are based on the present market price of wheat, $1 per bushel in Chicago. They are subject to changes of the market.

NIGGER WHEAT.
This is one of the best bearded, stiff strawed, No. 1 milling wheats for black and brown soils, I have ever seen. Grains very long, dark and hard. A very hardy sure-crop wheat. I particularly recommend this wheat for Southern Ind., Ky. and Tenn., where it has made very large yields. Sow 1¼ bus. per acre. **Price:** 1 bu. $1.75; 2½ bus. $4.00; 5 bus. $7.75; 10 bus. $15.00.

EARLY RIPE WHEAT.
This is a smooth wheat, red chaff. The straw is short and strong, stands up well on rich land. It is a very early wheat, and is not liable to rust or scab. The grain is round, plump and heavy and makes a first-class milling wheat. **PRICES:** One bu. $1.80; 2½ bus. $4.10; 5 bus. $8.00; 10 bus, $15.50.

HARVEST KING WHEAT.
This is a smooth red chaffed wheat, very similar to the Pool. It has a very stiff straw and is well adapted to strong, rich land. It is extremely hardy, in fact, I regard it as one of the hardiest and best wheats in the country. During the past three years we have had almost a failure of winter wheat in many localities, but the Harvest King has stood the test better than any other variety, and given in almost every case a fair average yield. Our seed is free from rye, cockle or chess. **Prices:** Same as for Early Ripe.

JONES' WINTER FIFE.—(Smooth.)
Chaff white, with a velvet-like glisten in the sun. Kernels very hard, dark and transparent presenting the same dark look when cut. From the dense nature of the grain it will weigh from 4 to 6 pounds more to the measured bushel than common sorts. It is especially desirable for rich, strong soils, producing an abundant yield of heavy, plump grain, requiring to be left until fully ripe before harvesting, as it does not easily shell in the field, and the seed improves in color.

Prices: Same as for Early Ripe.

Bags: Remit 15c for a new seamless bag, in which to ship each two bushels or less, that you order.

HOW THEY LIKE MY SEEDS.

I earnestly request you to write these parties, enclosing stamped envelope to insure their reply. If good reference be given me for their safe and hasty return, I will send original testimonials of any here printed, in their officially dated and post marked envelopes, to any who desire to see them. **A pleased and satisfied customer is my best advertisement.**

MR. GEO. BERRY, Dawson, Sangamon county, Ill., writes: "The corn I got from you was the best investment I ever saw on the farm. If you can beat it, you will have a dandy, sure."

MR. R. J. WILSON, Hyde Park, Ark., writes: "I have for some time been looking for a corn that would mature a good yield ahead of drouth. Your corn has proved to be all you claim for it in this respect, and just fills the bill."

MR. I. H. GOODNIGHT, Lancaster, Texas, writes: "Your corn is all O. K. here. It is 25 days earlier than our native corn, and will make all of 50 bushels per acre for me."

MR. G. W. PYLE, Colbert, I. T., writes: "Your Champion White Pearl matured 20 days earlier than, and yielded one-third more per acre, than native corn planted alongside. It is the best corn I ever saw."

MR. J. BAXTER ALLEN, Anniston, Ala., writes: "I like your Hickory King Corn. It is early, prolific, and almost weavil proof. It made a fine yield for me."

MR. ROBERT F. FISHER, Epperson, McCracken county, Ky., writes: "Your corn yielded as much on our poorest ground this year as our native corn did on our very best land. Myself and neighbors like it very much, because it matures ahead of early drouth."

MR. C. B. CHEATHAM, Murphy, Collin county, Texas, writes: "Your Champion Yellow Dent Corn made 37 bushels of nice corn per acre in 95 days from planting, or just 30 days before the drouth struck my native corn. My native corn being so much later, the severe drouth caught it while in the milky stage, and reduced its yield to 22 bushels of smutty corn per acre. I have made $26 clear on the half bushel of your corn this year over what I would have made had I planted all native corn. I have none for sale."

MR. JOHN D. COWAN, Austin, Kas., writes: "The corn I got from you matured 42 bushels fine corn per acre, two weeks before drouth struck my native corn, which made but 33 bushels; myself and neighbors much pleased with it."

MR. WM. ROE, Vinland, Douglass county, Kas., writes: "The 3 pounds of your Champion Yellow Dent corn matured its large, even, deep-grained, small-cobbed ears in 95 days from planting, and promises a large yield. Myself and neighbors are well pleased with it."

MR. J. W. FORD, Huntington, Ind., writes: "I planted your extra early yellow corn on June 4th. It fully matured in 90 days. I am much pleased with it."

MR. JOHN J. PAGE, Sparks' Hill, Hardin Co., Ill., writes: "Your corn far surpassed in yield my best native corn. I believe it is a very valuable corn for all localities subject to chintz bugs, as it matures before they begin damaging our native corn."

MR. E. D. SAPPINGTON, Nelson, Saline Co., Mo., says: "I take pleasure in informing you that I am satisfied that my yield per acre has been increased at least one-third by raising your C. W. Pearl corn. I fully endorse your way of doing business."

MR. OTTO KOMRO, Gilead, Neb., writes: "The Red Texas Oats I got from you last spring was much the earliest, very much the heaviest, and by far the best yielding oats in this country. My neighbors have offered me a big price for seed, but I will sow all I raised."

MR. C. H. BROOME, Charleston, Miss., writes: "I am highly pleased with your corn. It made very long and large well filled ears."

MR. BEN AMES, Mt. Vernon, O., writes: "I am greatly pleased with your corn. It yielded over 70 bushels per acre for me. Your manner of doing business is honest and prompt."

MR. J. L. LANCASTER, De Kalb, Tex., writes: "Your corn has given fine satisfaction, yielding one-third more corn to the acre than our native Texas corn. I like your way of doing business."

MR. BARTUS TRUE, Pomona, Kent Co., Maryland, says: "I am more than pleased with the corn I bought from you last spring. I like your business methods, and expect to patronize you in the future."

MR. J. W. POTTER, North Buena Vista, Ia. (80 miles further north than Des Moines), writes: "I am well pleased with your Champion Y. Dent corn. It will make about 75 bushels per acre of good sound corn for me this year."

MR. J. B. PIERSOL, Rockwell P. O., in Northern Iowa, says: "The Improved Leaming corn that I purchased from you last spring made me 62 bushels per acre, which was better than any of our corn from other seed. It is early, good-sized ears, kernels very compact on the cob, strong, sweet, and very oily. Stalks are very strong, and stood well. I attributed the extra yield to the change of seed, which I have always found to be of great advantage. I have no seed to spare."

MR. E. S. PARRETT, Jeffersonville, Fayette Co., Ohio, says: "I am well pleased with your C. W. Pearl corn. It is a fine meal and feeding corn."

MR. EDW. SMITH, Estaville, Ala., writes: "The corn we got from you last spring yielded 15 bushels per acre more for us than our native corn. Neighbors who clubbed with me say that they will plant nothing but your corn for next crop."

MR. AUG. KOENIG, Floyd, La., writes: "I am very much pleased with your corn. Planted April 3d; roasting ears June 15th. Fine large ears, and very large yield."

MR. LEE RICHARDSON, Vicksburg, Miss., writes: "I came out splendidly on the "Champion White Pearl" corn which you sent me last spring. I have never seen such fine corn grown here as your seed produced."

It is with renewed confidence in the superiority of my seeds, and greater assurance of my ability to render your investments in my seeds, as profitable and satisfactory to you, as theirs have been to them, that I again solicit your patronage. Believing that now is the time when they should have your careful attention. Yours very truly, **J. C. SUFFERN.**

BUY YOUR SEEDS OF THE GROWER.

Lightning Source UK Ltd.
Milton Keynes UK
UKHW051544240119
335965UK00013BA/1902/P